Horse Chinese Horoscope 2025

By
IChingHunFùyǒu FengShuisu

Table of Contents

Introduce

The character of people born in the year of the HORSE

People born this year like to talk, talk wisely, and have a lot of patience. You can endure any problem, no matter how difficult it is, without complaining in front of others. You enjoy making the best use of your physical strength. When you want something, you usually do it yourself unless you have lofty goals. Hardworking, not passive, always alert, enjoys being the center of attention, enjoys attending social events, participates in almost all sports, enjoys traveling, and enjoys competition. You are self-centered, despise conventions, and are cunning rather than clever. People born in this year value freedom, dislike being forced to do things they don't want to do, and are willing to give up everything for love.

Strength:

You get along well with others and are respected by them, brave.

Weaknesses:
You have a bad temper and frequently cause harm to others for no reason.

Love:
This year's babies are very attractive. Their love is not showy, but it is constant. It could be said that there are people who come almost every day to flirt and say nice things, and who would like others to come and take care of them. People born in this year dislike inconsistent people. A good-looking person with a narcissistic personality, on the other hand, is constantly thinking about how handsome or beautiful you are. People born in this year believe that they must be the only ones, so if you enjoy being pampered, you can be confident that you can permanently bind your lover.

Suitable Career:
People born in the Year of the Horse are fire-elemental, so they should pursue a career that matches their destiny, and their ability to

promote progress, prosperity, and profit. Education, research, occupation, teacher, doctor, administrator, beautician, gas station, photographer, shop selling stationery, all types of electrical equipment or handicrafts, selling artificial flowers, selling cloth, selling drugs, and creating publishing houses are all careers that will suit your luck. It was fated for you to be born in the Year of the Horse.

Year of the HORSE (Water) | (1942) & (2002)

"Military Horse" is a person born in the year of the HORSE at the age of 83 years (1942) and 23 years (2002)

Overview

For senior horoscopes, this year, your career and business will be smooth. There will be nothing for you to worry about. Therefore, if you have free time, you should find a hobby to do for fun, such as taking care of plants, and reading books, and you should take good care of your health, get enough rest, eat easily digestible and nutritious food, and do not worry too much about things that have not happened yet. And do not interfere or criticize your children, but be a shelter for them, and your life in the end will be happy.

For teenagers aged 23, this year, both in terms of study and work, there will be adults who will support and help you to find progress. There will be good news about auspicious work and fortune. If you increase your diligence and determination, success will be within your reach. However, you cannot underestimate the evil stars that surround your horoscope house, which will spread their influence and cause conflict and arguments among family members easily. When there is a lack of harmony, the house will not be peaceful. You should also be careful when using machinery that will cause you to be injured or bleed. In addition, you should be careful of accidents while traveling both near and far. When gathering with friends this year, be careful of being hit by a stray bullet. You should be mindful and discerning and not believe in the invitations of your friends who will lead you to places that you should avoid, such as pubs, bars, or nightclubs. You should also take care of your hygiene while eating because these will all be obstacles to your future work and education.

Career and Business

This year, due to the influence of the auspicious stars, whether it is education or work, the person will receive support from the elders, resulting in the advancement of the academic results. Or if you are working, your work will be supported by your superiors. Your boss will be fond of you and have the opportunity to be promoted. But be careful not to show off your skills. You should be respectful, and humble, and use polite words in communication. This will make your work progress even more. Especially if you are diligent, determined, and constantly improve your work skills to keep up with the changes, you will find a good starting point and a bright path. Especially during the months when your education and work will flourish and progress well, namely, the 1st Chinese month (February 3 - March 4), the 5th Chinese month (June 5 - July 6), the 8th Chinese month (September 7 - October 7), and the 11th Chinese month (December 7, 2025 - January 4, 2026). In addition, various investments are in good condition. The months when your work or studies will encounter problems are the 12th Chinese month (January 5 – February 2), the 3rd Chinese month (April 4 – May 4), the 6th Chinese month (July 7 – August 6), and the 9th Chinese month (October 8 – November 6). During these times, you should avoid investing because there is a chance of being cheated. If you start a joint venture with others, you should be more careful. You may be taken advantage of or cheated in accounting. In addition, signing a contract to accept work or employment or receiving a scholarship for further education must be carefully considered, and read the details carefully before signing a contract. Otherwise, it will cause problems in the future.

Financial

This year, your finances are quite good. Cash flow from salary and sales has good growth figures. You will have the opportunity to receive special bonuses from special jobs and windfalls. This year, if you have accumulated enough capital and dare to invest, the chances of receiving dividends will be relatively problem-free. Especially during the months when your finances will flow smoothly, namely, the 1st Chinese month (February 3 – March 4), the 5th Chinese month (June 5 – July 6), the 8th Chinese month (September 7 – October 7), and the 11th Chinese month (December 7, 2025 – January 4, 2026). However, you should be careful during the months when your finances have leakage points. Including unexpected expenses such as the 12th Chinese month (January 5 – February 2), the 3rd Chinese month (April 4 – May 4), the 6th Chinese month (July 7 – August 6), and the 9th Chinese month (October 8 – November 6) when you will face the problem of running out of money. Therefore, you should not lend money to others, do not guarantee for anyone, avoid gambling, do not be greedy for wealth that does not belong to you. You should also refrain from going out and spending money recklessly because besides not being beneficial, it also causes suffering in terms of money and health.

Family

This year, the family matters of this person are not very good. You should be careful about the health and safety of the elderly in the house. Fortunately, there are auspicious stars that support and promote, which can help reduce some of the disasters. However, you should not be careless or unscrupulous, especially during the months when there will be conflicts and unrest in the family, such as the 12th Chinese month (January 5 - February 2), the 3rd Chinese month (April 4 - May 4), the 6th Chinese month (July 7 - August 6), and the 9th Chinese month (October 8 - November 6). You should be more careful about accidents that will affect people in the house and the health problems of the elderly in the house. Also, be careful of valuables that may be lost, damaged, or deceived by criminals. In addition, you should not get involved in conflicts between friends and should distance yourself from friends who like to invite you to hang out and indulge in vices. You should also be careful of some friends who backstab you or often find ways to bully you to cause trouble and damage.

Love

This year, you will be especially charming. You will be liked by the opposite sex. However, you should remember that even though love may start with an eye for your appearance, love that will last is goodness and honesty. Therefore, you must know how to separate love and infatuation. Otherwise, the relationship will not last. The months when your love is fragile and problems will easily occur are the 12th Chinese month (January 5 - February 2), the 3rd Chinese month (April 4 - May 4), the 6th Chinese month (July 7 - August 6), and the 9th Chinese month (October 8 - November 6). You should not interfere in other couples' love affairs. Avoid going to entertainment venues and be careful of unintentional words that may cause arguments.

Health

This year, the health of both horoscopes in the age range is in the criteria that must be monitored because the health base has found a bad star to focus on. Therefore, you cannot be careless. For the elderly, you should be careful of health problems, especially clogged arteries, narrowed blood vessels, high blood pressure, and heart disease, and be careful of slipping and falling that will cause injury. For young people, you should be careful of accidents both during work and travel. There is a possibility of mourning for an elderly relative and getting sick. The months that both horoscopes in the age range must pay more attention to their health are the 12th Chinese month (January 5 - February 2), the 3rd Chinese month (April 4 - May 4), the 6th Chinese month (July 7 - August 6), and the 9th Chinese month (October 8 - November 6). In addition, you should be careful of illnesses caused by eating whatever you want and food poisoning. After a party, remember to "Don't drink and drive."

Year of the HORSE (Golden) | (1954) & (2014)

"The Flying Horse" is a person born in the year of the HORSE at the age of 71 years (1954) and 11 years (2014)

Overview

For senior horoscopes around the age of 71, even though this year the horoscope house will be surrounded by a group of bad stars, you are still lucky that during the year, two auspicious stars will shine and support you, which can help reduce some of the disasters. However, you should be careful and not be careless because your work and business will encounter obstacles and problems. In addition, work that involves using tools or machines must be extra careful because you may get injured or bleed. Be careful when walking on high or low ground because you might trip and fall. In addition, you must control your food intake in terms of quantity and hygiene. You should avoid cold foods and be careful of infectious diseases that enter through the mouth. You should relax, learn to let go, and not stress about your children, which will affect your physical health. For young horoscopes around this age, since the planets that are moving into the horoscope house this year are the "Thiang Tek" stars (the heavenly virtue stars), children will be loved by everyone in the house. In addition, their studies will progress. Therefore, this year you should study hard and review what you have learned to understand thoroughly. If you don't understand something, please study hard or dare to ask your teachers. This will help your academic performance reach your expected goals. But there are things to be careful about accidents while traveling and doing activities outside the home. As for making friends, parents should take care of them because there will be friends with bad intentions who will lead you in a bad way. Therefore, be careful and avoid them.

Career and Business

This year, the work and business of the senior is in good condition. Therefore, it is a good time for you to find an heir or assistant to continue the work and study and take care of new investments that are expected to yield the returns you expect. As for the education of the young person, this year there will be progress. If you are determined to be diligent, improve your skills, and gain knowledge beyond textbooks, you will progress even more and get better grades. You will also be liked by teachers and parents. In particular, the months when both career and education will have outstanding progress are the 1st Chinese month (Feb. 3 – Mar. 4), the 5th Chinese month (Jun. 5 – Jul. 6), the 8th Chinese month (Sep. 7 – Oct. 7), and the 11th Chinese month (Dec. 7, 2025 – Jan. 4, 2026). The months when your career will be hindered and have problems are the 12th Chinese month (Jan. 5 – Feb. 2), the 3rd Chinese month (Apr. 4 – May. 4), the 6th Chinese month (Jul.7 – Aug. 6), and the 9th Chinese month (Oct. 8 – Nov. 6). During these times, be careful of scammers. Do not fall for the lure of investment because you may be deceived.

Financial

This year, in terms of financial luck, you must be careful of losing money. This is because of the effects of the evil stars "Huai Yim" and "Suay Sua" that surround your financial horoscope. In any case, you should be careful of unexpected events that cause you to have to take money out of your pocket. Problems from illness or accidents are all causes of losing your money. Especially during the months when your financial star is low and unexpected expenses will come in, namely the 12th Chinese month (January 5 – February 2), the 3rd Chinese month (April 4 – May 4), the 6th Chinese month (July 7 – August 6), and the 9th Chinese month (October 8 – November 6). You still need to rely on careful financial planning and saving to get through this. In addition, you should have some money in reserve to prepare for unexpected expenses. The months in which your finances will flow smoothly are 1st Chinese month (February 3 – March 4), the 5th Chinese month (June 5 – July 6), the 8th Chinese month (September 7 – October 7), and the 11th Chinese month (December 7, 2025 – January 4, 2026).

Family

This year, there is a sharp star in your horoscope house, so you should be careful of injuries, bloodshed, and family members may have conflicts to the point of not looking at each other. In addition, you must keep your valuables hidden. Do not wear them to attract thieves, because you may be attacked and robbed. Therefore, please be extra careful, especially during the 12th Chinese month (January 5 - February 2), the 3rd Chinese month (April 4 - May 4), the 6th Chinese month (July 7 - August 6), and the 9th Chinese month (October 8 - November 6). As for relatives and friends, this year, older people will have the opportunity to gather with colleagues to make merit or go on a trip, which will make you feel happy.

As for young people, you should know how to distinguish between friends you trust and know how to reject friends who often invite you to go down a bad path. It would be better to invite them to do good deeds, study together, or tutor each other, rather than hanging out at the mall.

Love

This year, love and relationships will be smooth and bright. For the elderly, they will receive love and care from people around them. They will have the opportunity to take their partner on a trip or visit distant relatives, both in Thailand and abroad. This is considered a reward for their life that has been through thick and thin up until today. If they diligently pray and make merit, their life in their later years will be peaceful and happy. For the young people this year, even though they are loved and cared for, they must be humble. They may be mischievous like children and make mistakes. In this regard, adults must understand and gradually advise them with reason. Do not use emotions with children. Then, the children will behave better on their own. However, the elderly should be careful during the months when love is quite fragile and there may be some conflicts, which are the 12th Chinese month (January 5 - February 2), the 3rd Chinese month (April 4 - May 4), the 6th Chinese month (July 7 - August 6), and the 9th Chinese month (October 8 - November 6).

Health

This year, health is not good because of the influence of the evil stars, so you have to be more careful of injuries and take care of your health more. For the elderly, when going out, be careful of slipping and falling, which can cause injuries and bleeding. Don't be careless while traveling and picking up tools and equipment, and be careful about your drinking and eating hygiene.

As for children's health, this year, be careful of riding bicycles or motorcycles, which can cause injuries. Also, be careful of dangers from being involved with things that are hot and have flames, including electrical appliances.

The horoscope of both age groups must be more careful during the 12th Chinese month (January 5 - February 2), the 3rd Chinese month (April 4 - May 4), the 6th Chinese month (July 7 - August 6), and the 9th Chinese month (October 8 - November 6).

Year of the HORSE (Fire) | (1966)

" Traveling Horse" is a person born in the year of the HORSE at the age of 59 years (1966)

Overview

For the Horse horoscope of this age, this year is considered another auspicious year for you to have good things come into your life. You are another person who can organize a big birthday party (Tua Sai Yik) for your children to join in congratulating. Also, at the beginning of the year, if you like something, please decide to buy it to spend money to resolve the bad luck for the whole year. However, during the year, the evil stars "Tiang Sua" (heavenly disaster star) and "Suay Sua" (year disaster star) will appear to disturb your horoscope house. Therefore, this is another year that you should carefully consider your work or business before doing anything. Planning or doing any work should consider your readiness in every aspect.

In terms of finances, be careful of subordinates embezzling or stealing, and the problem of lack of liquidity of working capital. Therefore, planning your finances from the beginning of the year will help you deal with the problems that come your way without too much effort. It will also help your work proceed without any obstacles. In addition, the evil stars also cause health problems and accidents. Therefore, the horoscope should take care of your hygiene when eating and drinking. At this age, eating too much does not bring benefits but accumulates to cause harm, whether it is salty, sweet, or food that is high in fat. Too much of anything is not good for the body, whether it is diabetes, clogged arteries, heart disease, high blood pressure, obesity, or other complications. These are all threats to health and cause loss of wealth.

At this age, it cannot be denied that you are still as fit and strong as a young person. When your strength declines, if you work hard and do not get enough sleep, it may lead to injury or accidents. Therefore, this year, please be strict in taking care of your health. However, if there is an auspicious event in your home this year, it will be able to dissolve the inauspicious power of these two evil stars. Or you may find an opportunity to make merit by offering food to monks at home by placing the principal Buddha image facing north. This will help your work and obstacles go smoothly and help adjust your horoscope that is falling to soar again. In addition to creating unity, it also helps to dispel bad things.

Career and Business

The business of the person at the beginning of the year, because of finding a patron, will result in work progress. After the middle of the year, there will be conflicts. There will be problems in management both internally and externally. Therefore, the operations of work and business this year will require prudence and caution. If you plan to invest in any business, you should always have a backup plan, plan two, plan three. You also have to constantly adjust the work to accommodate unexpected events to prevent the business from stumbling in the middle. In addition, during the year, you should find the next generation to take over the work. This will help reduce pressure in many areas. As for the person in the horoscope, he will change his role to be a consultant who will stay behind the scenes and direct the work to proceed according to the plan. You will not be too tired. Entering the Chinese month 12 (January 5 - February 2), Chinese month 3 (April 4 - May 4), Chinese month 6 (July 7 - August 6), and Chinese month 9 (October 8 - November 6), you have to be careful of internal and external problems. During this period, please try to expedite debt collection from business partners or debtors and do not release additional accounts. Beware of bad debts, conflicts at work, problems with business partners, and beware of being deceived when making employment contracts or hiring. Also, beware of subordinates or partners embezzling or committing financial fraud. The months when work and investment will have a bright direction are the 1st Chinese month (February 3 – March 4), the 5th Chinese month (June 5 – July 6), the 8th Chinese month (September 7 – October 7), and the 11th Chinese month (December 7, 2025 – January 4, 2026).

Financial

This year's financial horoscope is quite good. There will be cash flow from two sources: direct salary or sales of products and services, or special money from special jobs such as bonuses, brokerage fees, winning the Government Savings Bank lottery, windfalls from gambling, or dividends from investing in gold or other investments. This is another year in which you can use the money to expand your business, whether it be adding more machines, factories, or branches, expanding sales channels, expanding production, or launching new products because this year is considered to have enough smooth time for the person. In particular, the months when the stars of fortune are bright and finances will circulate smoothly are the 1st Chinese month (February 3 – March 4), the 5th Chinese month (June 5 – July 6), the 8th Chinese month (September 7 – October 7), and the 11th Chinese month (December 7, 2025 – January 4, 2026). The months when finances will be stuck and have problems and unexpected expenses may interfere are the 12th Chinese month (January 5 – February 2), the 3rd Chinese month (April 4 – May 4), the 6th Chinese month (July 7 – August 6), and the 9th Chinese month (October 8 – November 6). During these periods, lending money, making loans, or being a guarantor for people close to you should be avoided. You must also be careful of scammers and you should not invest in illegal or immoral businesses.

Family

This year, even though you will find auspicious power visiting your home, at the beginning of the year, you should choose to buy valuable and desirable property to reduce bad luck. You should often worship the gods and deities. Make merit to reduce the bad luck from the evil star Suai Sua (the year's calamity star). In addition, you can organize a birthday party (Tua Saiyik) to use the auspicious power to break bad luck. In addition, during the year, you will meet good friends who will give you advice and help you survive the crisis. However, you should be careful of some months when your family will have problems and conflicts, such as the 12th Chinese month (January 5 - February 2), the 3rd Chinese month (April 4 - May 4), the 6th Chinese month (July 7 - August 6), and the 9th Chinese month (October 8 - November 6). You should find a way to protect your family members from injuries and be careful of losing money on medical expenses for illnesses of family members. You should also be careful of servants quarreling with neighbors. Be careful of damaging valuables. Lost or deceived by fraudsters. Also, you should not get involved in family matters or conflicts between friends. Also, be careful of some friends who will secretly harm or slander you, causing damage.

Love

In terms of love, this person's horoscope is moderate. The beginning of the year will be smooth, but after the middle of the year, arguments can easily occur. Entering the 12th Chinese month (January 5 - February 2), the 3rd Chinese month (April 4 - May 4), the 6th Chinese month (July 7 - August 6), and the 9th Chinese month (October 8 - November 6), you must be careful of conflicts and arguments with your partner because of other people's matters. Therefore, do not meddle in other people's affairs. You should avoid going to entertainment venues and control your behavior. Do not go astray. This will make you respected and honored by your children for a long time. Also, remember that a family is harmonious and peaceful. Therefore, if there is anything you can compromise on, you should compromise with your partner. This will help to make the atmosphere in the house more relaxed.

Health

Your health is not good. You must be careful of problems with your hands and legs. Heart disease, diabetes, high cholesterol, and high blood pressure will come calling. In addition, you should be careful of unexpected dangers that may cause injuries and bleeding, especially during the 12th Chinese month (January 5 – February 2), the 3rd Chinese month (April 4 – May 4), the 6th Chinese month (July 7 – August 6), and the 9th Chinese month (October 8 – November 6). You should be careful of the pain that may flare up. It would be better for you to go for an annual physical check-up so that if you find anything unusual, you can get treatment right away and it will be easy and smooth, and it will save you money.

Year of the HORSE (Fire) | (1978)

" The horse in the stable " is a person born in the year of the HORSE at the age of 47 years (1978)

Overview

For this age group, since this year there are groups of bad stars orbiting to spread influence and focus on you, you should not ignore health problems, especially accidents during work and travel. Be careful of injuries to the point of bleeding from using or being involved with tools and machines, including the dangers of falling objects from high places or slipping and falling. However, this year is a good opportunity for your work to find a patron, resulting in progress and opportunities for promotion. Your business will have opportunities to expand investment. Smoothness and success will be greater than damage. Various plans will pass without obstacles. Business will have a path of progress. Working or investing outside will have satisfactory returns. In addition, this year you will have the opportunity to buy expensive property or have the opportunity to move into a new house and expand your business. Therefore, it can be said that this year there will be a golden light of prosperity at your doorstep. Fame and money will come to make you happy. However, you must manage your finances and plan your spending carefully. Do not be extravagant as usual and do not spend money in the wrong way, such as investing in businesses that are at risk of breaking the law or spending money to party and go to entertainment venues. Because in addition to losing money unnecessarily, it will also cause you bad luck. Encountered trouble or accident.

Career and Business
This year, both your work and investment are quite smooth. You are likely to find a sponsor who is both a consultant and someone who helps and promotes you. Therefore, your business is on a path of progress. This year is a good opportunity to expand your branch, increase sales, acquire more businesses, or move to a new, larger office. For those who work regularly, there is an opportunity to be promoted. The months when your work will be

outstanding and prosperous are the 1st Chinese month (February 3 – March 4), the 5th Chinese month (June 5 – July 6), the 8th Chinese month (September 7 – October 7), and the 11th Chinese month (December 7, 2025 – January 4, 2026). In terms of collaboration or investment, this year will overall yield good returns. It is suitable for external investment to expand your base and manage your money for growth. However, you should be careful of some ill-wishers who may try to block or obstruct your work, causing trouble. Even though they may be minor, they can create big problems and headaches. Therefore, do not be complacent. In particular, the months when work will encounter obstacles and problems are the 12th Chinese month (January 5 - February 2), the 3rd Chinese month (April 4 - May 4), the 6th Chinese month (July 7 - August 6), and the 9th Chinese month (October 8 - November 6). Be careful of subordinates or juniors making mistakes and causing damage. If you do not hurry to fix it and let it escalate, it will become a big problem that will result in a lot of loss of property. Be careful when making employment contracts or hiring work, there may be minor details that will put you at a disadvantage.

Financial

This year's horoscope's finances are both gains and losses. The way to reduce the damage is to invest in businesses with low risks. However, overall, your investments in various areas are quite good. There are still opportunities and channels for mergers acquisitions and business expansions to be implemented this year, and there will be good results in return. However, you should be careful during the months when your finances will lack liquidity and unexpected expenses may interfere, namely the 12th Chinese month (January 5 - February 2), the 3rd Chinese month (April 4 - May 4), the 6th Chinese month (July 7 - August 6), and the 9th Chinese month (October 8 - November 6). During these times, you should not make new or additional investments because you are likely to be cheated. You should not gamble or take risks. You should not lend money to others or be a financial guarantee. You should not be greedy for wealth that does not belong to you.

You should not invest in illegal and immoral businesses because in addition to losing money, because you will be fined and punished, you may also have to face additional criminal liability. The months in which your finances will flow smoothly are 1st Chinese month (February 3 – March 4), the 5th Chinese month (June 5 – July 6), the 8th Chinese month (September 7 – October 7), and the 11th Chinese month (December 7, 2025 – January 4, 2026).

Family
This year, there will be good news about auspicious work and fortune. Many things will go smoothly as desired. In the house, there will be an engagement, moving out, moving to a new office, or there may be new family members. However, it is during the 12th Chinese month (January 5 - February 2), the 3rd Chinese month (April 4 - May 4), the 6th Chinese month (July 7 - August 6), and the 9th Chinese month (October 8 - November 6). Be careful of arguments and quarrels among family members. Be careful of losing valuables

or being damaged, or family members falling victim to scammers. Also, be careful when using tools and machinery, as you may get injured. Also, be careful of old or damaged fixtures. You should renovate, repair, or replace them. Be careful of falling and harming family members.

Love

This year, your love horoscope is good. You will be considerate and indulge each other. You can say that you can say anything you want, and you can say anything you want. You will never disagree. You are enviable. Even though you may have some conflicts or disagreements, they will not be serious. Therefore, it is a good opportunity for you to take your partner on a trip or make merit together to pray for blessings. This will help to add sweetness to your married life and also help to strengthen your love destiny. However, there are some months when you should be careful of conflicts and resentment, such as the 12th Chinese month (January 5 – February 2), the 3rd Chinese month (April 4 – May 4), the 6th Chinese month (July 7 – August 6), and the 9th

Chinese month (October 8 – November 6). You should be careful to control your temper and avoid triggers that may cause arguments. Also, do not get involved in other people's family problems. Also, avoid going to entertainment venues because, in addition to bringing conflicts, you may also bring back illnesses.

Health

This year, your health is not so good. It is due to the influence of the evil stars Huai Yim, Thiang Sua, and Sui Sua that are moving in to harass and cause health problems, illnesses, injuries, and bleeding from accidents. In particular, the months when you need to take close care of your health are the 12th Chinese month (January 5 – February 2), the 3rd Chinese month (April 4 – May 4), the 6th Chinese month (July 7 – August 6), and the 9th Chinese month (October 8 – November 6). In addition, you should be careful of high blood pressure, eating and drinking hygiene, food poisoning, gastritis, intestinal diseases, heart disease, clogged arteries, and silent diseases that may threaten to attack you. You should be especially strict

37

about eating and drinking hygiene. You should also be careful of accidents both while at work and while traveling on the road.

Year of the HORSE (Gold) | (1990)

" The horse is at the stable" is a person born in the year of the HORSE at the age of 35 years (1990)

Overview

This year, because your horoscope has a shining auspicious star, your career and business direction tend to change for the better under the condition that other factors are calm. Therefore, it is considered a good year for you to increase your diligence, develop yourself, and gain new skills to keep up with external changes. You should also visit your customers or those you have to contact regularly to build good relationships so that you can rely on each other and make your work flow smoothly. During this year, mistakes will inevitably occur in everything you do. Please remember that those who have never done anything wrong are those who have never done anything at all. Do not let the mistakes that have happened discourage you. When you know you have made a mistake, you should quickly fix it. Do not just make excuses. Improve yourself so that the same mistake will not happen again. In addition, there is something you should be careful about, which is trusting those close to you too much. This year, you cannot completely trust your relatives because some relatives do not wish you well as they say, but secretly want benefits behind the scenes. To make matters worse, some of them still have ill intentions towards you. It would be better if you kept some channels as an escape route for yourself. And the most important thing is not to get involved in internal matters or conflicts that may lead to lawsuits between friends.

Career and Business

In terms of work, this year, the auspicious stars will promote good people who are diligent in developing themselves. Your diligence and performance will be considered by your superiors for a higher position. Diligence in sales means that your business will grow in the future.

Especially in the following months, when your work and trade will move towards prosperity and progress, namely, the 1st Chinese month (February 3 – March 4), the 5th Chinese month (June 5 – July 6), the 8th Chinese month (September 7 – October 7), and the 11th Chinese month (December 7, 2025 – January 4, 2026). In addition, the criteria for working together and investing in various aspects are good. You can choose to invest in gold or increase your investment within or outside the business. Overall, you will receive good returns. But you should be careful during the months when your career will encounter obstacles, problems, and difficulties, which are the 12th Chinese month (January 5th - February 2nd), the 3rd Chinese month (April 4th - May 4th), the 6th Chinese month (July 7th - August 6th), and the 9th Chinese month (October 8th - November 6th). You should not invest in anything new or increase your investment because there is a chance of being cheated. You should also be careful of people who embezzle and cheat.

In addition, you should be careful that your work will make mistakes and damage. During the months mentioned, you should communicate clearly. When making a contract for employment or being hired, you should carefully consider the details of the contract so that you do not cause any serious problems later.

Financial

This year's finances for this person are "As you sow, so shall you reap." Do a lot and receive a lot of money. If you are lazy, you will miss out on money. Under the many smooth periods this year, please do not miss the opportunity to create results, and expand sales and income. If you have enough accumulated capital, you can choose to invest in new businesses. It will create pleasing profits, especially during the month when your finances will be bright and prosperous. And with good liquidity including the 1st Chinese month (February 3 – March 4), the 5th Chinese month (June 5 – July 6), the 8th Chinese month (September 7 – October 7), and the 11th Chinese month (December 7, 2025 – January 4, 2026). However, you should be careful during the following months when your finances will be hindered including the 12th Chinese month (January 5 – February 2), the 3rd Chinese month (April 4 – May 4), the 6th Chinese month (July 7 – August 6), and the 9th Chinese month (October 8 – November). Do not lend money to close people. Lending money, including guaranteeing should be prohibited. Also, do not invest in illegal or immoral businesses, including doing business or products that infringe on others' copyrights. Because in addition to losing property, you may also not be able to escape the penalty and have to be held criminally liable.

Family

This year, the family as a whole is still considered to receive auspicious power. Throughout the year, you will find someone to help and support you. You will have the opportunity to buy expensive property. There will be an auspicious time to move into a new place of work. There is also a chance to manage an auspicious event at home. For some families, there may be a few more members or a family member will receive a social position that is honorable and pleasing. However, you should be careful during the months when your family will have problems and conflicts, which are the 12th Chinese month (January 5 - February 2), the 3rd Chinese month (April 4 - May 4), the 6th Chinese month (July 7 - August 6), and the 9th Chinese month (October 8 - November 6). Be careful of valuables in the house being damaged or lost or members falling victim to scammers. Be careful of arguments with neighbors. In addition, you should know how to analyze and separate and distance yourself from untrustworthy relatives. Do not interfere in internal matters or disputes between friends. For relatives, this year is an average situation. Although there is a chance to find good friends who will support and help, there may be a chance to set up a big business together with a future. Or traveling together to observe works both domestically and internationally to bring back new technologies to develop the work that is being done. But one cannot help but be wary of some friends and relatives who are not pure-hearted and secretly harbor evil intentions.

Love

This year, love is in a good and charming category because your love base is influenced by the "Peach Blossom". Therefore, this year's love life will experience both good and bad things. On the good side, you will be very charming and will be popular with the opposite sex, possibly because of your good nature and good interpersonal skills. However, on the bad side, you must know how to be mindful and control yourself. Be careful not to fall into the trap of love that is not right, with the wrong partner, or to flirt with someone who is already taken. This will create bad karma for others. The months when your love life will easily have problems are the 12th Chinese month (January 5 – February 2), the 3rd Chinese month (April 4 – May 4), the 6th Chinese month (July 7 – August 6), and the 9th Chinese month (October

8 – November 6). You should avoid going to entertainment venues and be careful not to get involved with other people's husbands and wives.

Health

This year, your overall health will be strong and you will have full energy to work. However, you must not be careless with the disasters of the evil stars "Tiang Sua" and "Suay Sua", especially when working with tools, machines, sharp objects, electrical equipment or other machinery, or even cranes for lifting things in construction sites. Or you may be hit by objects falling from high places. Therefore, you should be extra careful if you have to travel near dangerous places, especially during the months that are not favorable for you, such as the 12th Chinese month (January 5 – February 2), the 3rd Chinese month (April 4 – May 4), the 6th Chinese month (July 7 – August 6), and the 9th Chinese month (October 8 – November 6), in which you must be mindful and control yourself. You must not be careless when driving on the road. In addition, be careful of diseases that enter through the mouth and diseases related to the digestive system. Most importantly, be careful of hidden diseases that may appear this year.

Chinese Astrology Horoscope for Each Month

Month 12 in the Dragon Year (5 Jan 25 - 2 Feb 25)

Your horoscope in the first month of this year is moving in a negative direction. It is a situation where you have to review past events. It is like riding a tiger once you are on its back. Therefore, during this period, the most important thing you should do is to meet and consult with many parties, both family members and people who are knowledgeable, about the current situation you are facing because many heads are better than one. Then you can gather your thoughts and evaluate your potential and abilities to see how ready you are. For any complicated plans, keep them to yourself before you announce a complete backup plan. Do not be impatient because if you do not set up the right management system, there will only be conflicts, which will be obstacles to future work development. Collaboration and investment this month are not going well.

For your finances, this month will be a turnaround. Income will decrease, but expenses will be overwhelming. You may encounter unexpected current expenses. In addition, when making a work contract, you should read the details carefully. If you are still not sure, do not rush to make a decision. As for collaboration or investment during this period, you should refrain from doing so.

Your family is in a situation of losing wealth. Be careful of subordinates or servants causing trouble and damage. Be careful of valuables breaking or falling victim to fraud.

As for love, it is in the moderate range. Let's give in to each other, no matter how heavy or light.

As for your health, during this time, you will encounter the evil star Kham Loet. You must be careful of accidents that may cause bloodshed. You must also be careful of food poisoning, colds, and other contagious diseases.

Support Days: 1 Jan., 5 Jan., 9 Jan., 13 Jan., 17 Jan., 21 Jan., 25 Jan., 29 Jan.

Lucky Days: 2 Jan., 14 Jan., 26 Jan.
Misfortune Days: 7 Jan., 19 Jan., 31 Jan.
Bad Days: 8 Jan., 10 Jan., 20 Jan., 22 Jan.

Month 1 in the Snake Year (3 Feb 25 - 4 Mar 25)
This month, you should prepare both Plan Two and Plan Three to support the new steps that you will take forward. Study and correct the mistakes of the past year to reduce the problems and obstacles of this new year. The most important thing you should do during this period is to build good relationships within the organization to gain cooperation from all parties to work smoothly. In addition, in terms of work and trade, during this period, you will find a sponsor, so there is an opportunity to expand work in new channels or come up with new ideas to expand from the original business. As for joint ventures or business investments during this period, it is suitable for investing in expanding work internally and investing externally. If you are ready in terms of people, capital, and plans, you can start. If you do it during this period, you will see good results in the middle of the year.

As for the financial horoscope this month, it is considered moderate. Direct income will still come in as usual. Although there will be some fortune, gambling and taking risks hoping for unexpected profits should not be expected too much. If you go all out, the damage will be great.

The family horoscope this month is peaceful. People in the house are loving and harmonious. Regarding relatives and friends, this month is quite good. If there are any obstacles, you will still receive cooperation and help.

As for love, it is still stable. Nothing is exciting during this period. But there is an opportunity to travel with your lover, both domestically and internationally. It is a time when love is happy and smooth.

In terms of health, you should avoid food that is grilled, roasted, fried, or baked, because it can cause the fire element in your body to be out of balance, which can cause illness.

Support Days: 2 Feb., 6 Feb., 10 Feb., 14 Feb., 18 Feb., 22 Feb., 26 Feb.
Lucky Days: 7 Feb., 19 Feb.
Misfortune Days: 12 Feb., 24 Feb.
Bad Days: 1 Feb., 3 Feb., 13 Feb., 15 Feb., 25 Feb., 27 Feb..

Month 2 in the Snake Year (5 Mar 25 - 6 Apr 25)

Entering this month, the horoscope of those born in the year of the Horse is considered to be in balance. For many things that are still pending, you can continue to complete them from the previous month because it will be smooth and good. In addition, in terms of work or business, during this period, you will find a patron to show you the way. There will be changes and new interesting avenues.

In terms of work, this month, there will be some changes to go to something new. You must have self-confidence, and dare to practice continuously to reach your goal of success. Because if you do not revolutionize and take action, you may have to follow others endlessly or may be eliminated or left alone.

Collaboration and investment will have a bright direction.

The important thing you should do during this period is, under other factors that are relatively smooth, you should strengthen good relationships with those you have to contact. When the budget is ready, combined with the ideas and plans that you believe in, this is a good time. When the water rises, you should scoop it up quickly. You must dare to put your plans into practice. This month's financial luck is moderate. Although normal income is still flowing in without any obstacles, there is also additional income from other channels running in. But because many expenses are due, you will not see the money. The important thing during this period is to Please not be greedy and hope for wealth that others bring to tempt you, you will find that you will lose wealth.

Family is peaceful.

Love is fresh and sweet. For those who are still single, this month there is a chance to meet the opposite sex that you have been looking for for a long time. This opposite sex will not only be interesting but will also help you with your work. For some couples whose love is ripe and perfect, this month is another good time to ask for love, both engagement, marriage, or moving out.

Support Days: 2 Mar, 6 Mar., 10 Mar., 14 Mar., 18 Mar., 22 Mar., 26 Mar., 30 Mar..

Lucky Days: 3 Mar, 15 Mar., 27 Mar.
Misfortune Days: 8 Mar, 20 Mar.
Bad Days: 9 Mar, 11 Mar., 21 Mar., 23 Mar.

Month 3 in the Snake Year (4 Apr 25 - 4 May 25)
This month, your horoscope is moving to encounter an obstacle, causing the horoscope line to lose its balance and become vertical. It is also affected by the power of the evil stars, causing your work and business to fall into a crisis with obstacles. What you should do on this occasion is to think carefully and find your flaws, find the cause of the problem, and quickly find a solution. Remember that even

though your work is being cornered, you should not give up. You should try to follow the second or third plan on a new path. In addition, signing a work contract or making any agreement that will have consequences must be carefully considered because there may be problems later. As for starting a job and investing in various matters, this month you should postpone it. If there is a meeting or socializing, you should be careful with your words. Also, during this time, be careful of friends betraying you.

Your salary will lack liquidity. Therefore, do not lend money to others or guarantee anyone. Most importantly, do not gamble because it may increase unnecessary expenses. Be careful of bad debt accounts and do not think of getting rich quickly by doing business that violates copyrights or is related to illegal things. If you are sued, it will make your financial crisis worse.

Family horoscope during this period, you must be careful of juniors causing trouble, be careful of arguments in the house, and be careful of accidents that may happen to family members.

As for the love horoscope, you will find a competitor. Therefore, you should ask yourself if this person is right or not. If so, do not be careless and let others cut in front of you. It is better to take care of your lover or spouse regularly so that you will not regret it later.

As for health, it is still a period to be careful of bloodshed from accidents both while working and driving.

Support Days: 3 Apr., 7 Apr., 11 Apr., 15 Apr., 19 Apr., 23 Apr., 27 Apr.
Lucky Days: 8 Apr., 20 Apr.
Misfortune Days: 1 Apr., 13 Apr., 25 Apr.
Bad Days: 2 Apr., 4 Apr., 14 Apr., 16 Apr., 26 Apr., 28 Apr.

Month 4 in the Snake Year (5 May 25 - 4 Jun 25)
This month, your fate will experience both good and bad things. In terms of work, even though it is still going smoothly and there is no progress, in terms of personal matters, there will be conflicts. You should be careful of illnesses that may attack you, causing your work to come to a halt. The most important thing you should do on this occasion is to find time to exercise and take care of your diet to strengthen your health. When you are assigned a task, you should quickly finish it and not ignore it.

In terms of work, be careful of chaos that may cause your work to be disrupted because people in your family are not united and there will be conflicts in your work line, and you will pass responsibility back and forth. When there is a lack of unity, it will be difficult to see results or sales.

For your salary, this is a moderate horoscope. There will be some direct cash flow and fortune. If you do not invest too much, you will have some left. As for investment, you should avoid it if you can because it will cause problems later.

In terms of your family horoscope, even though there will be problems, you will find a sponsor who will be your advisor and help you resolve obstacles. There will be a chance to take your family members on a trip or a long trip. For your close friends and relatives, remember not to get involved in your friends' conflicts. Beware of lawsuits.

As for love, you and your lover or spouse often have disagreements and arguments. Therefore, listen to anything and think carefully. Do not be gullible and believe those who do not wish you well. It will cause a rift. You should not interfere in other people's family matters. You should also avoid going to entertainment venues.

As for health, it is not very good. You must be strict and pay attention to your eating habits. Do not start taking care of yourself when you are sick. It will be too late and you will recover slowly. In addition, you should be careful of liver disease, high blood pressure, heart disease, and food poisoning. If you go out, be careful of accidents. During the trip, you may get injured or bleed.

Support Days: 1 May, 5 May, 9 May,13 May, 17 May, 21 May, 25 May, and 29 May.
Lucky Days: 2 May, 14 May, 26 May.
Misfortune Days: 7 May, 19 May, 31 May.
Bad Days: 8 May, 10 May, 20 May, 22 May.

Month 5 in the Snake Year (5 Jun 25 - 6 Jul 25)

This month, the horoscope of those born in the year of the Horse moves to meet the power line. In addition, there will be auspicious stars orbiting to shine and shine. Work will be smooth. Business will be prosperous. In addition, having good friendships and relationships with people around you at this time will be the driving force supporting your work and business to flourish and progress even more. The important thing you should do during this period is to be sincere and have good friendships to give to those close to you, including those you have to do business with, whether they are your superiors, subordinates, or colleagues.

This month, even though your income is good, you are likely to invest almost all of your money in one thing. In any case, you should manage to have some liquidity to save yourself. In case of emergency, you will not have to run around borrowing money.

In terms of work and business, this is a good time that you should not delay. Instead, you should hurry and work hard to move forward to your goals. During a smooth time, when relationships with people help dissolve the obstacles, this period will show good results and a lot of them. Starting a new job, investing in shares, and investing in various things, this period is suitable for starting something new.

The family is still smooth and happy.

In terms of love, this is a time to unite hearts. For singles, this is another good time to ask for love or reconcile during this good time. But for those who have a lover or partner, you should find time to change the atmosphere and find a place to talk about things that are on your mind with reason.

In terms of health, there will be no serious illnesses to bother or disturb you.

Support Days: 2 Jun., 6 Jun., 10 Jun., 14 Jun., 18 Jun., 22 Jun., 26 Jun., 30 Jun.
Lucky Days: 7 Jun., 19 Jun..
Misfortune Days: 12 Jun., 24 Jun.
Bad Days: 1 Jun., 3 Jun., 13 Jun., 15 Jun., 25 Jun., 27 Jun.

Month 6 in the Snake Year (7 Jul 25 - 6 Aug 25)
The horoscope has moved to a dangerous line, which affects work that is often obstructed and uncooperative. There are often arguments in the family. Therefore, the important thing you should do this month is to be mindful and calm

to reduce the hot temperature around you. Always check and take care of things that may cause danger to people in the house. You should also avoid the cause of arguments and conflicts among family members.

Your finances this month are moderate. Your income is stable. Don't expect luck because you will not have luck this month.

In terms of work, you still have to be careful of conflicts in the management line and conflicts with customers or those you have to contact. You have to ask for communication, coordination, and receiving any matters to understand each other so that there will be no problems later. In terms of working together, entering into shares, or investing in various areas, you should be very careful during this period. Before doing anything, you have to study carefully, otherwise you will be tricked by others.

In terms of family, there is a tendency for chaos because of division. What will help the house be happy is that the adults must be fair and dare to explain the reasons to those who do the wrong thing. In addition, you should be careful of family members having problems with neighbors. Be careful of valuable property being lost, damaged, or falling victim to scammers.

However, in terms of love, you have an auspicious time to do work, whether it is an engagement, marriage, or moving out. However, there are some prohibitions: You should not get involved in other people's families, otherwise, you may be drawn into a cycle of trouble.

For health, it is fair. During this time, you should be careful of gastritis, food poisoning, and gastroenteritis. This is another period where you have to be careful of injuries from accidents.

Support Days: 4 Jul., 8 Jul., 12 Jul., 16 Jul., 20 Jul., 24 Jul., 28 Jul.
Lucky Days: 1 Jul., 13 Jul., 25 Jul.

Misfortune Days: 6 Jul., 18 Jul., 30 Jul.
Bad Days: 7 Jul., 9 Jul., 19 Jul., 21 Jul., 31 Jul.

Month 7 in the Snake Year (8 Aug 25 - 7 Sep 25)

The path of life of the person entering this month, the direction of the horoscope is soaring, causing many obstacles that have accumulated to be resolved. The direction of work and business still has a good trend. There are channels and opportunities open to move forward. Therefore, you must use this time to move forward to create results and sales. Work hard and you will get a lot. Moreover, internal investments will have a good future. You will receive good cooperation and support. Various investments this month are good. There will be good returns.

The important thing you should do on this occasion is to think about others' feelings. Use kindness as a guide. Giving out will receive kindness in return. On a path that benefits each other, if you dare to do it, there will be an opportunity to lead others.

As for the salary, it is called bright. Income flows in from many sources. Both special work and regular work have satisfactory returns. But you must not be careless. It is better to save for the future and emergency flexibility.

The family this month is peaceful. People in the house do not have problems arguing or quarreling to tire you out. Relatives and friends will have a sponsor.

However, you should pay attention to your health because there is an inauspicious star, Khom Loet, moving to focus. For those who have chronic diseases, you must control your diet and exercise regularly. Avoid any conditions that will cause the disease to flare up. For those who do not have a chronic disease, if you experience any abnormal symptoms, you should see a doctor immediately to be sure.

In addition, you must be careful of accidents both during work and travel because there is a chance of injury.

Support Days: 1 Aug., 5 Aug., 9 Aug., 13 Aug., 17 Aug., 21 Aug., 25 Aug., 29 Aug.
Lucky Days: 6 Aug., 18 Aug., 30 Aug.
Misfortune Days: 11 Aug., 23 Aug.
Bad Days: 2 Aug., 12 Aug., 14 Aug., 24 Aug., 26 Aug.

Month 8 in the Snake Year (7 Sep 25 - 7 Oct 25)

This month, your horoscope will find a patron to help you. If you know how to learn from your mistakes, improve and improve, and increase your diligence this month, your work will find a path of progress. Businesses will sell well and make a profit. During this time, you need to increase your diligence and develop new skills for yourself. Do not be inactive. Most importantly, you should take good care of your work before reaching out to help others. You should also regularly survey the market, observe changes, and keep up with them. In addition, you will have the opportunity to expand your work and investments. If you do business, you will expand your business and production base. Trade and investment will have a good growth direction.

For your finances, this month, there will be a cash flow from things you have invested in, both from your regular job, salary, sales, and extra money from additional income.

In terms of family, this month is peaceful. You will have auspicious wealth visit you. You have the opportunity to buy valuable property for your home. Relatives, siblings, or friends will visit each other and help each other well. They will always give you useful advice. If you have encountered obstacles and problems in the past and do not know who to turn to, try talking to your relatives or friends.

In terms of love, this period is like a fish in water. Your lover is attentive.

This month, my health horoscope is good, with no complications.

Support Days: 2 Sep., 6 Sep., 10 Sep., 14 Sep., 18 Sep., 22 Sep., 26 Sep., 30 Sep.
Lucky Days: 11 Sep., 23 Sep.
Misfortune Days: 4 Sep., 16 Sep., 28 Sep..
Bad Days: 5 Sep., 7 Sep., 17 Sep., 19 Sep., 29 Sep.

Month 9 in the Snake Year (8 Oct 25 - 6 Nov 25)

This month, your horoscope will be surrounded by inauspicious stars, causing your horoscope to fall and lose its center. Your work will face problems and obstacles. The most important thing you should do this month is accept work and make any contacts. During this time, you should communicate clearly. If there are conditions and time constraints, you must assess your existing capabilities to see if you can handle it and meet the deadline. Do not be stubborn or show off your skills because this month, if you encounter any damage, you will look for someone to help you. It seems that no one is around.

In terms of work and business, during this period, you will encounter "competitive stars". Therefore, you cannot be complacent with your business competitors. It is better to plan carefully and prepare a plan two or three or look for new markets and channels to deal with.

In terms of finances, this month, you will be in a situation of financial leakage. Therefore, you must be careful about spending. Do not gamble or take risks. Do not do businesses that infringe on copyright or violate the law because you may face criminal charges. Do not lend money or accept guarantees. Be careful of problems with liquidity problems corruption in accounting and bad debts. In addition, you should delay investing and expanding new work. Do not rush to invest during this period. Keep looking for the right time for the next opportunity.

Family horoscope is another period that you have to keep an eye on and be careful of injuries, and bloodshed from accidents and there is a chance of losing valuables. Relatives and friends during this period may have to keep their distance because there is a chance of being deceived.

Love's horoscope is experiencing a storm. Going to entertainment venues, be careful of catching an illness.

As for health, it is not so good. During this period, you have to be cautious. You should be careful of accidents during work and travel. In addition, you have to take special care of your health. If you find any abnormalities, you should see a doctor for a thorough examination. You should also be careful of high blood pressure.

Support Days: 4 Oct., 8 Oct., 12 Oct., 16 Oct., 20 Oct., 24 Oct., 28 Oct.
Lucky Days: 5 Oct., 17 Oct., 29 Oct.
Misfortune Days: 10 Oct., 22 Oct.
Bad Days: 1 Oct., 11 Oct., 13 Oct., 23 Oct., 25 Oct.

Month 10 in the Snake Year (7 Nov 25 - 6 Dec 25)
This month, your life path will encounter an unsupportive month. Many things that you expect and intend will have a change. But if you are diligent, determined, prepared, and do not let go, you will be able to make up for the lack. What you should do during this period is to be calm, and composed, and think before you act so that you can overcome unexpected events. In addition, you should use humility to solve personal problems.

Your finances are quite unstable. Therefore, you should reduce unnecessary expenses and frequently check for financial leakages because if you are not careful, you will immediately run out of liquidity. In addition, you should not get involved in any form of gambling and risk-taking. Reduce financial risks by not lending money or being a guarantor for anyone.

In terms of work, you will encounter conflicts at work again. But if you use politeness to handle bad things, you will be able to handle them. Your work will still progress. However, during this period, you should think carefully about investing in various areas. You should ask experts and find information from all sides before making a decision.

During this period, your family horoscope is still blessed with auspicious energy. Even if there are conflicts at home, they can still be managed. You just have to talk slowly, use the time to meditate, and be patient.

This month, your love life is in the middle range. There may be some problems of resentment, but they are not serious.

In terms of health, be careful of gastritis, enteritis, and liver disease. You should also be careful of accidents both inside and outside the home. Therefore, during this time, you must be mindful of everything you do. If you are not careful, you may encounter danger.

Support Days: 1 Nov., 5 Nov., 9 Nov., 13 Nov., 17 Nov., 21 Nov., 25 Nov., 29 Nov.
Lucky Days: 10 Nov., 22 Nov.

Misfortune Days: 3 Nov., 15 Nov., 27 Nov.
Bad Days: 4 Nov., 6 Nov., 16 Nov., 18 Nov., 28 Nov., 30 Nov.

Month 11 in the Snake Year (7 Dec 25 - 4 Jan 26)

The Year of the Horse's life path is rocky and shaking this month. It's because your fate has progressed to the point of malice. As a result, the destiny graph plummeted rapidly. Work, especially business, is similar to being tested and meeting issues and hurdles. Things were introduced one by one. You should avoid interfering with other people's tasks this month. To be safe, you need first to take care of yourself. You should also manage your money and have enough cash in your wallet. Strange tasks, luxury projects, and easy money are considered twice before undertaking them. Furthermore, if there is a tale, it is not required to be conveyed. Both should be able to communicate well with others. Understand how to be modest and courteous. Do not be arrogant or intimidate less fortunate people.

In terms of fortune, this wage is not favorable. Income began to decline, failing to achieve the objective, and debtors became difficult to collect, with some incurring bad debts. Meanwhile, costs are rising. As a result, you should not gamble or sign financial promises to support anyone at this time. Avoid becoming entangled in criminal activities. Because there is a potential that a lawsuit may be filed.

In terms of jobs, be wary of swindlers and cheats that take advantage of you. Every action is carefully planned to be a trap. Before signing any contract agreements, you should carefully verify the details. In terms of families, be wary of people in the house arguing with each other and pay attention to home safety.

Stormy waves wash over the loving side. You should be able to regulate your emotions properly. Your health is in poor shape during this time. Be wary of heart disease, liver illness, and diabetes. Please maintain proper drinking and eating habits. Starting a new career, investing in stocks, or making other investments this month is risky and should be avoided for the time being.

Support Days: 4 Dec., 8 Dec., 12 Dec., 16 Dec., 20 Dec., 25 Dec., 28 Dec.
Lucky Days: 9 Dec., 21 Dec.
Misfortune Days: 2 Dec., 14 Dec., 26 Dec.
Bad Days: 3 Dec., 5 Dec., 15 Dec., 17 Dec., 27 Dec., 29 Dec.

Amulet for The Year of the Horse
"Gods of Wealth, Hok, Siu, Spreading Wealth."
Those born in the year of the Horse this year should set up and worship the sacred object "Thep Hok Lok Siu Sap Phae Pai San" to enhance their destiny. Place it on your work desk or cash desk to ask for the power and influence of the three deities to help enhance your merit, fortune, wealth, and long life to the person of your destiny.

In one chapter of Advanced Feng Shui, it is mentioned about the deities who will come down to reside in the Mie Keng (House of Destiny) of the year, which are deities who can bring both good and bad things to the person of your destiny that year. Therefore, worshiping to enhance your destiny with the deity who comes down to reside in the same year as your birth year is considered to have the best results and have the most impact on you. To use the influence of that deity, to help protect you while your destiny is declining and having bad luck to alleviate it. At the same time, ask for blessings from them to help your business and trade run smoothly as desired, and bring glory and prosperity to you and your family.

Those born in the year of the Horse or Mie Keng (House of Destiny) are in the sign of Ngow This year is a year that will bring good results to you even though you will face high pressure and competition in your career. But luck is still on your side because the auspicious star will encourage you to find a patron. Business will have a path of progress. Collaboration and external investment will have satisfactory returns. In addition, the person in the horoscope is likely to move into a new house or buy expensive property into the house. There is an opportunity to expand the business and improve your status. There will be a light of prosperity visiting the door of the house. Fame and money will come in. But because the horoscope has the evil star "Huai Yim" staring in the zodiac, you should not overlook the health problems of you and your family members who will get sick. There may be dangers from using tools and unexpected events that cause injuries and bleeding. Beware of being a victim of fraud. The person on the horoscope must be more careful of accidents during work and travel, including taking care of their own health and family members more closely. Love is more exciting than a roller coaster. You and your lover will be in love for a while, and then become sworn enemies. As for general health, it is good, but sometimes there may be problems with the digestive system because of accumulated stress and insomnia this year. If you want to solve and alleviate the disaster, you should set up and worship "Gods of Wealth, Hok, Siu, Spreading Wealth" to ask for the power and prestige of the three gods to help promote the career and business of the person of the horoscope to be prosperous, progressive, the goods circulate smoothly, fortune and wealth, good health and the family are safe and secure and full of happiness. Hok, Siu, is a symbol of the three gods in the Poj Seian process or the Eight Achievers. It is considered the highest auspicious blessing that will help promote the person of the Horse year to be complete in everything they hope for. "Hok" comes from "Hok Khi" (the left god), meaning good fortune, power, honor, stability, and wealth with assets, as well as being complete with children, servants, and a partner. "Lok" comes from "Hong Lok" (the middle god), meaning fortune and wealth, complete with assets, that is, being complete with consumer goods, gems, silver, and gold, and being complete with servants, having children, and a good partner. And some people use "Xiu" from "Xiang Xiu" (the right god), which means longevity and good health.

In addition, those born in the year of the Goat should wear a lucky pendant in the shape of "God of Wealth, Fuk, Xiu" around their necks or carry it with them when traveling outside the home, both near and far, so that the person will be filled with auspicious wealth and properties, have prosperity and progress in both business and trade and have a peaceful and happy family throughout the year, resulting in better and faster efficiency than before.

Good Direction: Northeast, Northwest, and South

Bad Direction: North

Lucky Colors: Red, Pink, Orange, and Green.

Lucky Times: 1100 – 11.59, 13.00 – 14.59, 19.00 – 20.59.

Bad Times: 05.00 – 06.59, 09.00 – 10.59., 23.00 – 00.59

Good Luck For 2025

Manufactured by Amazon.ca
Bolton, ON

42642145R00046